AF416915

while i watched the airplanes

To the stranger at the airport that fateful day,
and Shannon

CONTENTS

Departures

Turbulence

Check-In

Airplane Spotting

Departures

Brain Cancer

They brought in a buzzing choir to fill the quiet,
To sing hymns and discourage me from her-
esy. The MRI commences, and they scan for the
growth.

I was administered blood tests and given pills,
With bread and a 5 ml spoon of wine to replenish my
strength, post-test.
They gave me old books to reference for self-care tips.

My identity became my diagnosis.

Screens flashed, speakers beeped, numbers hollered,
chairs screeched.
I'm 0316, awaiting payment.
Consume once before food, and again before sleep. I
give thanks.

Leaving the pharmacy, I sanitize my hands to rid the
bacteria inhaled. The sun outside is a lot warmer.
I feel converted, anew. Healthy, no longer askew.
My Sunday's almost over. I feel giddy — my head
hurts, my vision's blurred. Throw up a little.

Perhaps my delirium is acting up again; hopefully
treatment is effective this time.

Jack of Hearts

Foolish, loitering adolescents
Craving to experience the thrill of young love,
Laid out and giving away their firsts,
Like a rookie's game of poker.
The house is full, body count two, but to feel being
filled comes with emptiness later.

Come back, Jack
Blackjack, hit twenty-one. Or she never did, and
settled —
Cheeks flushed, identical hearts —
For the picture card with the loose moustache,
disheveled,
But with the bad boy impression she adored.
(Or for the bejeweled Jack of diamonds who should've
been denoted the Jack of asses.)

Unaware of the Ace, with more than just a suit to
match.

But forgone, forlorn, flippantly folded,
The Queen of Hearts cashed all in, foolish, loitering,
And to divorce from her chips, left a bankrupt, single
mom.

Smothered

Honey, I know you by heart, from your viscous
Nectar, to your hearty indulgence in cream,
Sugar, candied apples, and your caramel

Skin —— gorged yourself thin.
Gorgeous girl with her pink
Fizz and sparkly cocktail

Dress, bejeweled like
A Christmas tree,
Ruby heels,

Velvet
Skin,
And hair so dense she can't hear the pounding music
from within.

Stomps
To my side,
A hippopotamus,

Sliding her sticky arm
Through the vacancy in the
Nook between my forearm and forehead.

Interlock, tug
Of war.

She hollers at me, commenting on my reticence and
restraint.

My arm a snake, slithers away from her drunken
grasp. While I do yearn, I refuse, persisting in living
vicariously

Through the sardines drowning in syrup
(spotlighted by ominous red, green and blue),
downing more cups
(dyed in dazzling red, green and blue).
She retreats from the leper into the shadows.

Self-control remains the anchor of the ascetic;
strangulation of the stoic; power source of my
psychological static. In it I find satisfaction in the
stasis.

Honey, I don't know your heart.

Beautiful

The curb was my balance beam, and with toes curled
and arms outstretched like a flying copter, I resisted
the vertigo, preventing myself from slipping into the
grass patch, that was lava. Then I saw her, the little
blossom bursting from center of a cluster of Ixora,
clad in red, frail and tempting. I stepped down from
the curb and into the unknown, hunched over, and
stared.

She was beautiful thing.
And I wanted to pluck her from the roots, just so that I
could keep her forever,
Because perhaps, I wanted keep her forever out of the
hands of mother nature, to consume her nectar,
destroy her, and let her rot — to devoid her of love.

She was a beautiful thing
And I was the seasonal transition that would cause its
petals to fall; its stalk to wither. All I had to do was
arrive. All I had to do was send a breeze, until it was
swayed by me.

Two Adventurers

For every time they embarked on an adventure,
It was a journey to you, but a treasure hunt to me.
Perhaps it was rude to be searching for someone,
something else
While being with someone, something else.

I showed you the alleys I knew too well:
The nooks, corner shops, hidden gems,
And gave you the same diamond encrusted,
counterfeit necklace I'd given others before,
To swing around your neck like a leash.

I helped you discover
Rainy days, sorbet
Seven-hour conversations, and other clichés.
I continued to search beyond you.
Easy, easy.

I led
Following my moral compass that spun and spun,
Uncertain, a twinkling, quivering Northern Star that
the two adventurers relied on.
I pointed out the constellations,
Spouting about horoscopes and affinity
Until you murmured, *"we're soulmates"*.

Did you forget I lacked a sense of direction?
How were you so convinced when I feigned awe
At sights I've seen before?

Your demise was plotted, planned, by the fraudulent
astronomer.
I guess the only truth I told you was that I was a
Cancer.

Mary Rose Sat On a Pin, Mary Rose

I promised to never put you into a rose,
Thumbelina, for you would slip
into the xylem pipelines and drown in my guilt.

I swore that after the ninth hour, I would gaze
Beyond your baby face and towards the three days
Of rebirth and roses.

Yet for three years I transfixed and transgressed
As Mary contracted and conceived —
A child I exalt yet neglect.

Child, I waited like a child.
Holding onto hands and handfuls of sweet
Nothings and imaginings; insatiable longing.
Workings of my mind, geared towards producing a
perfect package
Of potpourri, to penetrate the pungency of loneliness
with the saccharine sweet

Lingering

Smell of cheap perfume, that diffuses through the
room and reminds me of you
And a brothel.

Magpie

Magpie rumored to adore beauty
and lust after pretty, pretty, pretty
stupid things.

Mi amor, I've flown around you for far too long —
I've let you pick at my brain and snatch whatever
gems your nosy self desires.

Princess obsessed with diamonds and oblivious of
her curse of entitlement,
Feed me happy pills of your smiles and empty praises,
Overpour dopamine, trigger the receptors.
Make my birdbrain reliant on your superficial smiles,
Your sugar coated, sickly sweet charm; your thick
syrup of ignorance.
Darling, my wings are weighed down, too heavy to be
the owl for your late-night sobs.

At the sixth hour we may have met, and I made the
mistake of stepping further into your embrace,
To discover that the dimness of your mind is too dense
to bring enlightenment, despite your pretty face.

But within I found a shadow of my being, a glint of
selfishness to thieve, and proclaim that
I will not be the eagle in your valley, or the Jesus in
your Gethsemane — make your penitence elsewhere –
The grass flowers I stumble onto within the valleys
have never been worthy of being stabbed into my
bouquet.

Princess, you are displaced, juxtaposed by the
Queen of the Night.

Watch

"I am a broken watch."
In the process of fixing
The scratches on my face turned to dents,

In the process of retuning
Myself to present time,
I fell further behind.

The mechanic's hands fondle mine before he snaps
Them off. Sir, why do you tell me not to self-pity
when I'm frantic?
Don't you know that sends me into a greater frenzy?

Engineer my mindset, sir.
It's been years, since
Tick

Tock
We talked. But my silence doesn't mean time stops…
Did my warranty really expire?

Ringgg!

The different rooms happened long ago
When nothing changed and our hearts grew cold.
For we were waiting, for something not coming:
The illusion of hope, a godsend, a miracle.
Where things fixed without pliers,
Tightly secured without screwdrivers.
Too much faith in the wrong places.
Faith, in each other's guilt, trips them like untied laces
That never stopped coming loose, no matter the knot
tied.
But like how fires don't ignite without a spark,
We're cold in the dark.
And we wait in the quiet.
Just to think, maybe we just got tired
Of the presence we saw every day,
The ups and downs, the whole display
Of raw emotion, unfiltered, explicit and rogue,
An endless cycle, with no real goal.
What now? The point of dating was to marry,
And thereafter, to carry babies.
And die. That'll die. It died.
Vows said in pure affection,
Mission complete, dissolution of motivation.
We wait for each other to give in,
We wait for time to pass,
We wait for the regret,
We wait for guilt,
We wait for this,
We wait for that,

We spent the whole time waiting,
We forgot about the time we had.

Two Souls

But even with insoles I keep slipping
Up and I can't help sometimes
But sing the wrong tune, and buy the wrong shoes,
and sit you down on a broken chair
To talk
About feelings and introspection, languages I feel in
braille
While I sign back to you with yearning in my eyes,
confusion in my fingertips, and empty words on my
lips.
The deaf speak incomprehensibly, articulation unclear,
Then trying again and again, to fulfil their duty,
wishing that they could decipher words from the loud
scream of silence.

It's okay, your blindness was more important anyway.

Bread

A fleeting thing. The feeling
Through your nose as your airways contract; the feeling
of your breath weighing down on your diaphragm.
The weight.

The weight of appreciation yet responsibility
for the lights outside that were turned off at two but turned on
again, at six in the morning.
The weight of breakfast foods wrapped in tin foil,

Love weaved into carbohydrates, and
Slathered onto wholegrain.
The weight of hating kaya toast but having to force it down my throat any way,
Because of the weight.

-

"You go first, I'll catch up with you later!"
Under his shirt, impregnated with a secret
Hidden beneath his forearms.
He clasped his elbows, and pressed securely against
his tummy, as a mother would her newborn child.

Waddling and with a sheepish smile, he sneaked past the intruding gazes
To the front of the classroom and towards the corner.
He loomed over the bin and lifted his shirt

And out emerged his bagged secret.

A squashed slice of wholemeal bread.

A hollow thump as it hit the pit, into the darkness and
never to be seen again.
Mission accomplished.
Emancipated, he took off in a sprint,
The weight of cut crusts off of his shoulders.

"Wait up guys! I want to buy food too!"

Are There Any Good Men Left?

Well, Tommy Boy here, would beg to differ
In his bright blue boots and football dress, he sprints
for the goal in high-heeled swank.

When did, with knowledge, come the ambition and
passion, that sets man afoot on their stairway to
heaven?
Believing that they were capable of conquering cities
and constructing Babel; capable of working behind
closed doors to attain whatever their hearts desired.
Because all we need is passion! Love! Joy in what I
do, and then the feel good!

I pity the spouse who has to bridge the gap with a
single rib, from the ground to your serenade spitting,
sickly sweet mouth.
Screw her deeper into the ground, as your head rises
so far beyond your feet, that your neck can't connect it
to your body.

We gave you apples and we snatched the drug, but
how did you end up the one
Entrapped in the moon?
In your cage of ambition and filthy pride, sons shoot
suns, like their ancestors would've liked.

Out, the last light that bedazzles the sky, the spotlight
that focuses on your black tongue, murmuring careless
whispers dismissed by your ignorant laugh.

And how dare you police me with your closeted envy,
a K9 bearing canines with greed?
You belong on a leash! The poor darling, you have
convinced and fooled, to parrot your cacophonous
broken tune back to you.
Your gentlemanly gestures a facade for your failings
to be as accomplished as your father; your smooth jazz
to serenade and intoxicate the unsuspecting girl.

Your perverse, threatening, unaccepting mind, that
hides behind your false faith in the transience of time
That success waits at your door, like a mission to
unlock, and if you gain enough experience, you'll
evolve into a striking hawk — for god's sake awake!
Playing your video games, slumped on a couch,
twiddling your thumbs to shoot the ball that's gone
out.

You're on the outfield! A red card, Tommy, for your
angst:
Your violence, sliding tackles, and underhand
Insults used to manipulate, as if you could
psychologically control the flying ball.

Boy, you missed your penalty kick! Goddamn move
on!
Stop playing games with your net of tunes, an
entanglement not a mellifluous complexity, rather a
messed mongrel's misinterpretation of their muse.

Run within your penalty box, even when the ball is not
in your court, chase your dreams and score!

Into your own goalie's hands.
Missed the target once, you'll miss it again,
If you don't descend
Your spiked boots from your high horse, drugged up
on ambition and your dazzled friends.

Arrived

The blue sign flickered. The melodramatic wind began
hollering. Headlights glared into the dark tunnel,
illuminating it in jarring yellow, prophesying of The
Arrival.
It rode on rails as if they were palm leaves,
announcing its presence with incessant beeps.
We looked away and at each other,
"The next one, okay?"
Unspoken, but following the same train of thought as
we remained stationary, stubborn as mules to leave
with the rest of the congregation.

The countdown restarted, "7 minutes".
We had sat down at half past six, but now it was long
past rush hour.

We spoke in intervals and in turn, never interjecting
each other, alternating between speaker and
listener, speaker and
listener. Topics
Came and went.
Came and went, and we continued waiting for the next
coming.

Then the time came
We stood up and the doors opened and you went forth.
I watched the doors close silently.
We looked away from each other.

Can We Still Be Facebook Friends?

We lived in a snow globe. During some periods it
rained full stops,
Usually when dawn broke and the sunlight reflected
off the shiny surface of the glass. Good morning
Or good night? We've been staring at the glass for 6
hours now
Or more? I lost track of time…I'm exhausted but I still
want to talk to you…I lost track of time; you make me
laugh…
Likewise, hey! I'm blocking you on Facebook,
stop laughing at my childhood photos.
You look so different (you're so cute here though)!
Shut up. Stop shaking the glass
I want to make it snow! But the snow is melting in the
sunlight
It's okay it's poetic (— did I ever tell you I love your
writing? It's so good it makes me wonder) did you
copy that line from somewhere?
Uh why? Does it suck?
It's a little cheesy.
Oh I (wrote it even though it seems like I) copied it
from somewhere.
No wonder.
Oh ok. I'm blocking you on WhatsApp, Snapchat, and
Instagram.

Hearty!

An afterthought. A sweet burst of flavor, dense,
tongue taut, but
Tongue-tied when probed too deep, like the bone in
your sandwich —
Stabbing you in the gut.
Why

Do we consume with beings that do not scare? The
parasite in your
Dessert that leaves your stomach bare. And why
Do we falter like frail, shriveled beings,
When asked to reveal the meat between our bread
skin?

Vegan! Fake carnivore!

She recites the ingredient lists of her leafy leaving
friendship circles.
Touching bases, brushing surfaces, thumbing crusts.
Decomposing cucumbers, molding bread,
And yet she revels in the crumbs of small talk and
non-nutritious gossip.

She licks the plate and marvels at her grand ability of
cleaning it up —
The only thing she has ever done.
Indulging in napkins and plain rice,
Bland and processed like the ketchup on her knife.

I observe the patron unable to appreciate

The delicacy of rich conversation.
Instead, slithers of food sprawl out on the rich girl's
plate.
She looks at her French buffet, satisfied by the
commonplace and titters.
She teeters away from the tête-à-tête

Un-sandwiching herself by leaning into the plain but
safe side.
And so, we picnic, her fake friends and I,
Busking together in the superficial sunburst
Of adrenaline and time.

Toblerone

Regardless of the perpetrator:
We grew out of each other.
We reached the peak and admired the sunrise. Then,
the only way was down, back to the summit,
Of which I snowballed toward, excited to conquer
other mountains,
Leaving you behind to sip your hot cocoa that I had no
interest in because I like my chocolate dark and solid.
How ironic is it, that our conversation on the way up
was fueled by talks of ambition to conquer future
Everests?

Yet now we drift, me, pulled by the alpine breeze, and
you, stagnant in the comfort of your apathy's cell of a
hug, of which I broke through, while you submitted to,
sipping hot cocoa.

50 Shades of Yellow

He arrives, unannounced, slips in quiet, he's in *my*
house.
Packaged nice, fabric tight, donned a
plastic foil suit and twist tie.
Whisper sweet nothings, as I pucker up, mesmerized,
you tantalize, your shirt- I untuck.
Yellow skinned, origins, of exotic Thai places,
Autumn, spring, re-emerging, momentary physical
pleasure.
Enter me, slide over my tongue,
Taste buds in a tango, your kisses, I love
How the aftermath, leaves me, longing for more.
Thereafter, you linger, as I stroll through the corridor
In my mind, yearning, for a second time
To be in that sanctuary, a moment still, that I wish
could last forever.
This fruitful affair with the one I love
My man
Goes.

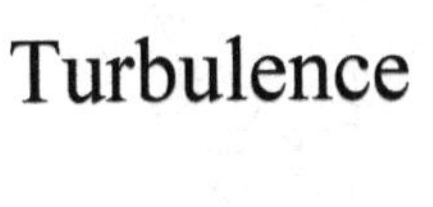

Turbulence

Harvest Season

Disease of the mind, chicken
Pox, strawberry skin, pores
Like sand, scattered, many,
Like constellations that glare
and flare, red and staring,
Bright, confronting, accusing,
"You did it again."

Chicken soup, black and herbal
To cure the disease of the mind,
Stomach, and soul. Popcorn skin,
Gritty, rough like sandpaper,
Unsmooth, uncouth, scarred
And red. Acne-red. Broken spots,
Overflowing, unkempt moss.

Trails, hanging, like the gardens
Of Babylon, tendrils circling,
Entwining, coiling and shaped
Like nooses. Dangling. Ripe fruit,
Tomatoes, red spots, strawberries,
Soft. It's harvest season.
Pluck!

Picked off the ripe, lengthy, stretched
Stems, tweezed from bumpy furrows;
Along irrigation paths that split at the ends,
Crowded by fauna — a pair of hares from
The same hole. Snap! Ensnared. Rabbit
Soup, chicken goop. Chicken stock,

Pop rocks, white Crocs with black socks,

Chicken spots — chicken pox.

HONK!

Let's be friends, Miss Crazy Eyes.
I want to get to know you — impulses *and* tendencies.
Let's run off into sunsets,
Onto roads and dare people to kill us. Then scream,
"HONK!" back at drivers when they horn at us.
We're invincible, Crazy Eyes.

They can't destroy our souls, we're magicians.
Come with me, we have nothing to lose if we've
already lost it. Brandish that machine gun you bought
just for fun.
Let's make this dirty death a gorgeous nightmare.
So pretty.
So pretty.
Your eyes are so pretty, Crazy Eyes.
I like staring at them when you stop speaking.

Knock, Knock!

Crazy Eyes, are you home this evening?
I could come in for a side of milk and honeyed
cookies,
Whist reading pretentious poetry
About mentally unstable adolescents, and narrations of
their mess in retrospect!

Come in, it's been a little lonely
In my empty house of three.
The rooms have been filled with ghosts, and the
echoes of the bones buried years ago.
Sometimes they still scream something about
cognitive dissonance.
I guess I failed to silence them completely or reconcile
with them — I shouldn't have kept their bodies intact.

I'll sleep on the concrete tonight. That area with the
hatchet buried. Hopefully, it will put me to sleep.
If you weren't here I might've been staring out at the
moon, awaiting epiphany; ignoring my revelations.
Praying for transcendence despite my transgressions.
"Come find me, enlightenment!"

My dilemmas have crowded my cupboards, and my
sink is flooded with worry, choked by the hair balls
down my throat. Sorry this place is a little
dysfunctional, it's from the pulling and scabs...

It's okay, Crazy Eyes. Tonight, we have each other, it's the company that matters, not the appliances. Good night, Crazy Eyes.

"Good night, darling."

Dear Aunt Amber

You smell like antiseptic, and look like death in a
dress.
You appear to be the visual representation of the
chronically depressed.
Was it the miscarriage that led you to Miss Crazy
Eyes?
I believe you found each other, when your fetus died
And was ripped out of your future, after being
nurtured and maintained,
Life breathed into it but I guess the positive's now in
vain.
For what is borne of you, is the futility of the hopeful.

Aunt Amber, you're a stock drop, an impending death
of a cause,
Neither prophets nor witches could have foresaw.
Aunt Amber, aren't you the reincarnation of ill fate?
The victims who, an ambulance crashed into, whilst
trying to save your child? The hollowness in your
womb
serves as a reminder against all projections of your
future.
It has been gnashed by teeth, and shredded by the
claws of Miss Crazy Eyes, but you don't remember.
It's fine. Responsibilities don't matter.

Yours Sincerely,
Miss Crazy Eyes, your babysitter.

Rendezvous

It feels like February 17th
again, when I held your long,
callused fingers, and you
grasped my neck, and pulled
me deeper into you, and I felt
your breath, and I knew, that
if I pulled any tighter, any
closer into me, I would
obliterate out of existence.

Your nails drag against my
skin, peeling it back, flesh
taut and you, taunting, me to
proceed in letting you enter
me. Because you knew you
were addictive, and that I
loved your hushed whisper
against my ear; lingering kiss.

But I released you.

Fear

Sometimes, I get scared. Fearful. Uncertain. I don't draw my curtains, because I'm afraid the flies may penetrate my safe haven. I get scared. I get scared that I won't ever settle, that my heart won't be full even when I think I've found something that makes me happy. Or so I think, when I project my imagination and break from reality with my shards of romanticism, away from the realization that I am just a small being with many great ideas I cannot execute. And I pray my hardest, and hope I will be kept safe; from the soles of my feet to the crown of my head.

I repeat this nightly, the way I repeat myself now, and continue my trend of thought with polysyndeton and repetition, reiteration, but make a turn with conjunctions which function to represent change. The beginnings of questioning my devotion to spacemen and space travel; stuck in a limbo, under a pole, which cuts my neck if I dream too high above the reality that follows, but breaks my back if I fall below the surface.

Either way, the forcefields keep me away from the otherworldly that I balance between my human hands and human eyes that hope and hope and hope to see.

Exorcism

You were exiled but you brought back 6 other friends;
but don't worry it's an open invite, no RSVP
necessary!
Come, all ye faithful, sit at my dining table for supper-
I'll sit on the dinner table.
Gnaw me away — sinner parts.

Crumpled like tissue — do you know what it feels
like?
Pinned like an animal, restrained, pulled, pushed
Deeper into the ground, and wishing you could
dissolve
And give it what it wants — your descent into hell.
Slow,
Evolving, knees buckling, hands slapping
The floor, clapping
Together like a hysterical seal, laughing like an alarm
clock, gone off
Like my head, off hinges, like my joints, snapped.

But unlike my jaw, left hanging, screaming, wordless,
wishing I could go louder,
Louder. Infestation, manifestation, evolving within,
into a thousand leeches, gnashing fangs into my bone.
And I fight back as I'm told. Even though it's easier if
I don't.

The hysterics, the emancipation, the grand release, the
final blow,

The black shadows, gore and cannibalistic darkness,
consuming.
Do you know what it feels like?

Submission and laughter, masochism —
You'll hurt me as I'll do you, then sympathize and cry,
Satisfy and grieve.
A symbiotic relationship.

Penitence

Some days I just delve in the guilt, as if my pain
would alleviate yours,
or perhaps it's my selfish means of comfort, and to
create an opportunity for indulgence in more self-
loathing. I pray you don't remember and couldn't
process; I hope you don't view those nights like I can;
I wish you don't think back at all. Please forget. Never
reminisce.

Thrice this month I was asked about my biggest
regret. I'd reply something politically correct: like
social media, or that my mind's blank…
"I'll tell you later," I haven't gotten back to them yet.

Sorry. I did to you what was done to me.
If I ever have the courage to confess, if I'm indicted
and serve the due sentence:
I hope you don't understand the charge, I hope you
don't remember.

Animals

The opportunist closes the gates, gazing out
Longing for the beasts that lurk beyond the freedom of
Eden.
"I was brought up better than the animals that roam in
the wilderness," he mutters,
Consoling himself, that what will be gained is greater
than what has been lost.

Caged, he debates with himself
And justifies how the walls keep him safe.
Knowledge (of good and evil) allows
(good and) evil doing.

The crossroads of sacrifice confront him.
He stalls at the junction convinced,
There will be a ram.
There will be a ram.

And we'll pray that he doesn't get rammed,
Headbutted by sideview mirror horns.
The sheep in the headlights stares into enlightenment
right before the crash.
Decapitation may just be his emancipation.

Drowsy

How do I awaken from this daze of despair?
Diagnose my narcolepsy for fear that I collapse back
into
this
slumber
of haze that blinds me; of fog and filthy air that
clouds me, the dagger that distracts me, and the
ambition which leads me, towards the particles that
coalesce into the crowds that surround me, in the
loneliness and desolation which follow me
into tomorrow,
to tomorrow,
tomorrow.

Until the flame engulfs my being, before briefly
dissipating into smoke, going
Out, Out, Out,
I will be a player, and present my show,
In hopes that none of my audience awakens
from the anesthesia.

Check-Ins

Checkpoint

Tiresome. Annoyed, half-heartedly chopping
passports.
Wheels turn, and roll when beckoned — faces blank,
too tired,
Grey under the pink light of dawn. Exhausted
Spirits wait, retired and resigned to patience.

Breathing bodies, in, out,
Waiting, breath not bated, but beaten.
Driving in, windows down,
Glance, compare, glance, compare.

Chop-chop, signal, next.

Besieged by the stream of moving boxes, the
Mechanicals assess the mechanical,
Both driven to move, motioning forward.
Hence these motions: glance, chop, chop.

The radio's on, but still broadcasting white noise.
Nonetheless, the wheels on tarmac
Interrupt the tranquility, screeching, scratching —
reveille!
The gantry opens, impatient driving onto the fast lane
And he steps on the gas, faster, faster,

Maybe this way it can be over quicker, over quicker,
Accelerating and gripping the wheel, feigning control
As he returns to the quicker motions,
Into the red, the mundane.

Playing Fields

In the eastern wing of the world, resides misguided
children,
who believe their path is straight.
But a bird from above
would squawk about a roundabout
with a singular exit, blocked by metal gates, letting in
only those slim and agile enough to
squeeze
through
the
gaps.

In these mazes and spaces, the children interact with
the robot kids, admiring their shiny coats and cutlery,
Silver spoons tucking into the 7-course meal of pride
and glory made by daddy.
On the odd playing fields, the children stretch forth
and hurl their bodies to pass milestones, pushing like
Sisyphus
While the robot kids gaze
down from above, uninvolved, as the mud would
tarnish their polish.

When the sky goes dark, the children slip back into the
cracks
of
their
dorms, rolling into bed, and praying fervently, that
they would encounter ladders over snakes — a wishful
matter of die.

They hide in the corners to keep them safe tonight. In
adjacent rooms, the robot kids plug back into the
safety of the net.
They rest soundly, for the rest of the night.

Integration

Can't we be numbers?
Some positive, some negative, and despite the
difference between those significant and insignificant,
they all still make up a figure. A digit less, and values
plunge.

Conundrums may arise.
There would always be quantities, which would
attempt to divide, to convert and log you into a certain
result. But the power in numbers is what gives even
the unknowns value, as long as there is equal balance.

even the most long-winded, complicated, and
irrational numbers are aided
By the ones in their circumferences who round them
up, discovering their significance, and assisting their
pointless circles of problems.

Can't we be numbers — a billion, zillion, but not one
left behind…alas.
But pi in the sky.

Subway

While waiting for trains,
I timidly confessed my insecurity
About your wealth and my greed.
As we discussed the future, I tried
To balance my ambition with your security,
While my mother balanced jobs,
And my father combatted sleep.
The other day before waiting for
Trains, that man approached me,
asking for your number like I wasn't
pretty — pervert pursuing sixteen-
year-olds at twenty-three. And so
I busked in the alluring glow of your
Billboards, like a moth, a parasite,
And splurged on foods my allowance
Didn't allow. But by the end of every
Masquerade, we would still be waiting
For trains that headed in different
directions — to your private estate
And my humble abode. Then the
Automated onlooker would remind me,
"please mind the platform gap."

Airplane Spotting

Acrylics

Plaster me to the fridge as I vandalize the popcorn
walls of my abode.
Shred my canvases of young pride and ambition;
drown me in turpentine and flood my brain with fumes
—

My sustenance.

Purge the emotion that drives me to pursue a
beautified path of blood and gold,
For the satisfaction of having my name engraved, on
graves that may quote me with hopes to
Have been the difference. To
Be worth the remembrance, and exaltation.

I am a mendicant who clings to the coattails of your
curiosity, wishing a penny for my thoughts.
My priceless, depleting ideas are a lucid flow,
trickling down my frail state of mind —
Encapsulating, letting go.

To fuel, I feel,
My neurons pulsating
Thoughts ricocheting past perceived potential paths of
paint and pain
But never to materialize.

Explicit Content

Treat me like a photograph, a Polaroid, if you will.
Unique, individual, cut me open, and I'll spill
Ink blots, extracted by gravity, dripping in a random
motion,
Trickle down, your curious fingers, stained by the
unknown black potion.
Our faces would fade, from the surface, of the
pigmented film to form
An asymmetrical Rorschach's test.
What incomprehensible mess of a monster do you see
now?

Filter my speech, hide the expletives.
Lower the exposure, prevent me from being explicit
With my thoughts, and my emotions,
Saturate my joy and lower the temperatures of my
sadness.
Increase the vignette on my peripheries,
Frame my silhouette.
Apply lens blurs —
Make me the subject.
Lastly, caption controversially to contrast:
 (a) *unique* (individual).

I'm a special snowflake, short and touting,
Here is my handle, where I spout.

Beauty to the Blind Beholder

They write about waves and sunsets and flowers
And about running through expansive fields, like their
words in these blank spaces.
They talk about freedom, romanticism, and the
juxtaposition of life and death, working down their list
of popularized themes.

Once they have decided, the creative process begins.
Thumb up, thumb down; thumb up, thumb down.
Tap-tap-tap.
Alas, the final product is complete.
In the glory of serif typography, the one-liner reads:
"Today I am sad."

Yet I must admit, the succinctness does capture
My resignation to the culture
Of black screens white text, white screens black text,
"(*What's happening?*)"
With an additional sign-off
— *reiterating their names*.

I pity the idea,
entrapped in a 280
character box, with
what's captured but
a caricature. Hearts
and thumbs for all!

MINIMALISM

Big eyes big ears big hearts big mouths.
We see we hear we feel we say,
But what exits is filtered, and what they see is the
sheer epidermis, clean shaven, smooth, naked. Devoid
of
Visual auditory olfactory emotional verbal capacity.

The Machine

Mark-making into skin, stippling
To amplify the tonal contrasts:
Between the sunshine and sweater weather; good and
evil; life and death; pretentious and earnest.
Bleeding out the last of the toxins, her diagnosis has
been beautified. With the permanent reminder, she
labels herself as a respected felon who overcame.

We, the vandals, stain temple walls, ruining the
celestial city with our lack of decorum and distasteful
decor — idealized, romanticized crimes.

We wear our sins on our sleeves like badges of honor,
as if confidence and aesthetic would mask the tragedy.
And with the old-fashioned, we debate
Between facades of perfection for dignity's sake,
Or a mark signifying the human condition of unending
mistakes.

Unartistic

In a system of people-machines and machine-people,
we find satisfaction in innovation and conduction,
where both are quintessential in the construction and
clockwork of function and progress, to execute and
ideate; where "too many machine-people" doesn't
exist.

This manic frenzy is described in the art that we
create,
where we form obnoxiously poetic, perfectly polished
pieces of commentary on society and its mishaps. We
simultaneously sell out, causing

Our art to lose its authenticity when we are no longer
capable of understanding our own cognitive processes,
because there is nothing left to express and explain.

So how do we talk about nothingness?
Jargon. The previous stanzas embody this as I give
into my flow of conscious and muscle memory and no
longer think.
I just write in flowery language, punctuated by little
blooms of trisyllabic words, and ensure that my
punctuation and repetition create a rhythm and rhyme
scheme that sounds a bit like a metronome with a
shouting machine in the background.
A bit like a mumble rap with a drop and squeaky,
unpolished, polka-dotted electronic sound, composed
together with a pretty album cover to portray the
illusion of commercialism and good, high, art.

But what the hell is an artist without inspiration?
And what the hell are creations without meaning?
These are lifeless, hollow shells
That once held bullets, but now lost in the
aforementioned war of modernity.
Oh, how pathetic and self-pitying is this loathing of
the system that keeps us in place but leaves me
displaced.
The machines don't have the time of day to entertain
deviants!

Self-centered, entitled bitch,
You are the failed creative that only speaks bullshit
And hollers, "JARGON!" masked by
confidence, charisma, and color.

Where is the Ground?

Let failure be that sobering reminder, the sediments in
your mental bank
That the world is not your oyster, and that few would
bother
To dig deep for the pearl beneath your pebble
appearance.

Let the soil penetrate into your roots, and be the
grounding factor to your fleeting, wildest dreams:
The sharp rocks that puncture and deflate your pride;
The attrition that wears down your ambition.

This is the emancipation from the hot air
Discharged into fantasies of the could haves, should
haves, but did not.
It is the potential, the buildup,

The suspenseful peak, and the falling
Action, that drives us into desolation — the
denouement.
Perhaps this is growing up.

No longer a Little Mermaid, toying with bubbles and
the idea of discovering Atlantis
Now a fish out of water, flopping, flailing
For a pair of lungs and feet.

OTEL
ADE
TFK

About the Author

Dorothy Yuan is a Visual Arts student from Singapore who spends her train rides writing. In her art, she navigates the liminal space between modern culture and the past, using her work as a platform for sociopolitical commentary. However, while some of these themes do translate into her writing, her poetry tends to observe the more intricate relationships between and within people. Her poetry has won the All In! Young Writers Festival People's Choice Award, while her art has been showcased in exhibitions and published in magazines. At the end of a long week, you'll find her lost in thought at the airport viewing gallery watching airplanes.

Acknowledgements

While I Watched the Airplanes was written between 2015 and 2020, during the prime of my teenage years. It was written mainly in the gaps of time I had travelling from place to place, be it by bus, car, or train. It was my outlet after a long day of classes or events, for the emotions only expressible through the abstractions of imagery, and for the emotions I couldn't just plonk out on the screen of a blank Instagram story. These emotions were captured in the moment, and the poems are the byproducts of me taking the time to process and phrase them into words.

The book has been split into four sections: Departures, Turbulence, Check-Ins, and Airplane Spotting. These are symbolic of one's relationships with others, self, society, and art, respectively. While many of the poems have been written with specific memories and themes in mind, a few are also just meant to be fun, simple explorations of puns (see *50 Shades of Yellow*, *Integration*). I hope you had a good laugh (or partially amused exhalation) while reading those.

The title of the book alludes to a Sunday afternoon after church, when I spontaneously decided to head to the airport viewing gallery to read. The cover design was inspired by a photograph from that day. I ended up conversing with a middle-aged man sitting across from me, who was waiting for his flight back to the States. As we talked, I found out that he was a music teacher who had travelled to Singapore to teach an orchestra. We bonded over the joys and struggles of loving and doing art, and the conversation ended when he had to leave. This is a special memory because it was one of the first times I had approached a stranger for the sake of getting to know them. Likewise, it's the perfect metaphor for this book, reflecting the risks and impacts of getting to know something or someone. Additionally, to me, airplanes also symbolize the ambition, freedom and hope in youth. Thus, it felt especially apt to ironically end with *Where is the Ground?* which presents the polar opposite. While an extent of hope is necessary to keep one going, it is as equally important to be grounded in reality. And I guess discovery of that balance has been my indicator of growing up.

First and foremost, I want to thank Shannon Chow for being the only person other than myself to own a copy of the very first draft of this book. It was bound by hand with thread and my mediocre sewing skills, and cut horribly using a pen knife. Thank you for always encouraging me to write, and expressing how much you enjoy reading my writing despite how angsty and unpolished it was back then (and sometimes, even now). Thank you for being the perfect balance of constructive and kind with my art, and honestly one of the few reasons I bothered self-publishing in the first place.

I also want to express my gratitude for the many people that have helped me create this book one way or another: my fifty or so Instagram followers who religiously watch my Instagram stories, reply to walls of reflective text, and affirm my writing abilities; my editor Vanessa Dreams for her honest feedback; my parents for giving me the freedom since young to explore the depths of my imagination and for encouraging me to pursue my goals (ha dad, I published a book before you!); and all the friends who have seen me evolve and grow as a person through the years, putting up with my bad puns, creative outbursts and sudden periods of radio silence (which often, just meant I was lost in thought or asleep).

Last but not least, thank *you* for getting a copy of this book. It has been written, illustrated, and designed from scratch by yours truly, and it means the world that you (or someone who cares about you) decided that it was art worth paying for.